WHAT REALLY COUNTS

The story of Cara, a Very Preterm Birth survivor

August Irons

ISBN 979-8-218-21636-8

Sky Island Signature   Wolcott, Vt
USA

I was entering retirement in good health, feeling quite satisfied with my life and myself …. except when it came to intimate relationships. I figured retirement would allow me to delve more deeply into that aspect of my life.

Excited to tackle my bucket list, I would first get rid of all the things I no longer needed.

one

She called in response to my listing in a local paper: *Gold Tone banjo for sale*. Her voice was that of a preadolescent girl. Though interested in acquiring the instrument, she hesitated to set a time to see it. I figured she had to work it out with her parents and told her I would be willing to hold it for her for ten days. After three phone conversations over the next two weeks and still no commitment, I informed her that I could no longer hold it for her. "The banjo should go to someone who *has* to have a banjo," I said. There was a long pause, then in a barely audible voice Cara said that she would come to see it the next day.

It was beautiful though chilly that next day when I stepped out of the barn to see a low-riding '63 Chevy Impala SS slowly making its way in my badly rutted

half-mile-long lane. I watched as I walked
toward the cabin, expecting that Chevy to
get hung up at any moment, but the car soon
pulled up to the cabin and the young driver
got out smiling. I knew it had to be Cara.
"I'm impressed," I said, "maneuvering that
car in here like you did." She glanced at me,
then stared at the ground. "I have taken that
car back many-a-road just as bad," she said.
I said nothing, and she began shuffling a
pebble about with her foot. She was bundled
up as if it was January, in over-sized
Carhartt overalls and a puffy jacket with
hood drawn. I waited for her to look up, but
she just kept her gaze on that pebble. I could
only see a face, one that would have had me
guessing whether she be boy or girl was it
not that I felt sure she was a girl simply from
her voice. I turned to her Chevy. "I'm
jealous," I said. Cara glanced up then and I
thought she appeared pleased.

   We talked for a half hour without the
banjo being mentioned. Cara appeared to be
more interested in knowing how I was
running the farm off-grid. Her curiosity was
endless. I realized that this modest girl who
still had not made eye contact more than a

fleeting glance, was in conversation incredibly agile, moving flawlessly to wherever it turned and revealing at every shift that she carried a virtual encyclopedia in her head. Yet during the whole of that conversation, she was still working that pebble.

I offered to make tea, and she smiled. Suddenly she looked at me, then threw back the hood. As a physician I instantly noticed the absent ear lobes, mild frontal bossing, and microcephaly. I had earlier noticed a fleeting gesture undeniably odd, but other than noticing it, had made little of it. There was little doubt in my mind that she bore the misfortune of genetic and developmental abnormalities. To see such an affected one be so dexterous in conversation captivated me. "Let's step inside," I said, "I believe I have some shortbread cookies to go with the tea, if you'd like?"

"Yes!" Cara replied, "Thank you, I love shortbread cookies!"

After tea, I suggested she look at the banjo. Cara willingly examined it but appeared to be more interested in our exchange. As if she sensed my awareness of what she lived with, she began to share bits and pieces of her history. Suddenly she turned to the banjo, saying "I'll take it", and pulled out a wallet.

"Put your wallet back," I said, "the banjo is yours."

Cara smiled, eyes glued to the floor, and in that little girl voice said, "Thank you." She stepped out the door, banjo in hand, and without looking back said in a barely audible voice, "I would like to see you again."

I watched as she maneuvered that old Chevy out the lane. Things she had said swirled in my head. And memories. My brother Rob had driven an identical '63 Chevy SS when we were teenagers. Cara somehow reminded me of him, beyond the wheels. Rob had been not only a brother but my best friend as well. He was killed in a motorcycle accident while he and I were cruising Skyline Drive. We were in our twenties then, and already had our lives planned out

two

Cara said "sure!" when some weeks later I called saying I was going to visit a friend and would be passing her way, and did she care to have dinner with me? I confess that I was relieved upon arriving at her apartment and saw that she was not dressed like a boy - though it bothered me a bit to think it mattered. As we walked the two blocks to Anjour's Bistro, I mentioned that people were likely to think I was her grandfather. Cara laughed and asked if that was ok, and I answered that yes, that I would prefer they do. She laughed again, as if that was funny.

Anjour's was crowded, with most of the folks hanging out around the bar in an adjacent room. Cara and I were happy to be seated without a wait in the main dining room away from the noise. After an awkward five minutes in which Cara struggled to decide what she wanted from the menu, we settled into a non-stop exchange of life stories. Her story was dark and incredibly sad; it poured thickly down over my heart, and I had to fight against tears. I remember thinking that there was something more than mere co-incidence in our paths intersecting. I summoned our waiter for a second glass of wine. He suggested we might move to the bar to free the table, for we had been there nearly two hours. We thanked him for his patience and left. Cara pointed to a bench in front of the adjacent railroad station. We sat there until we were shivering, then walked back to her apartment. Cara asked if I might stay the night. I replied that I had planned to stay at a motel because I should be heading out quite early. She said I should stay, that she would be up and have coffee and bagels with me as early as I wished. I said ok. We sipped wine and talked long into the night. Somewhere around two I retired to her couch, exhausted but unable to sleep.

It was mid-morning when I woke to the smell of coffee. I rose, stiff and groggy. "Not very early," I mumbled.

"You didn't specify a time, nor did you ask me to wake you," Cara replied as she handed me a cup of coffee. "Anyway, I knew you were lying. I'll fry some eggs if you'd like." I smiled, and Cara laughed. We ate by a window looking out over a little garden in the back yard. A pair of mourning doves called from a bare limb of the lone pine standing between the garden and a vacant building pocked by missing mortar and broken brick.

"See the doves? Joe and Suze," Cara said. Then she waved to them, and I did too.

three

A week after our dinner date Cara called and asked to visit, wondering if she could stay for a few days and help on the farm. I said, "Sure, come on up."

Cara was eager to see the farm, so I suggested that we go for a walk. After having tea, we pulled on our boots and hit the first pasture. It wasn't long until Cara began to lag behind, repeatedly calling out for me to slow down. The more I slowed, the slower she walked. It appeared that each time she came across something of interest, she would stop and not move until I stopped to wait for her.

Cara stayed for a week. It seemed to me that she was injecting a kind of sideways romance. I simply did not know what to do with that.

Some weeks later I called Cara to inquire how she was doing, and upon learning that she was scheduled to undergo an outpatient surgical procedure, I offered to take her to and from the hospital. She was quite pleased, saying she was looking forward to seeing me then. The day prior the procedure I emailed her, asking what time I should pick her up. She promptly replied that another friend was taking her. I expressed my displeasure that an agreement had been broken without first communicating with me about it. Her response was that I had major problems, that I was jealous, immature, manipulative, pathetic.... it went on as if once started she could not stop. I did not reply. Two days later I received an email from her that was casual and friendly. There was no indication in it that she thought anything unusual had happened. Again I did not respond. The next day I received a flurry of emails and phone messages from her, sounding fraught with fear, saying repeatedly "something's wrong, and I want to know what. You can't just treat me this way. I can tell you're pulling away. You're just like the rest of them."

I waited two days, then replied, explaining that I had never had a friend turn suddenly hateful and assassinate my character when I but voiced a grievance.

Her response was "Well, you deserved it, you needed to be put in your place. It's called hard love."

That floored me.

four

After a few days of questioning whether I really had it in me to continue with Cara, I called and suggested that we spend a day together driving around the countryside, take in a few shops, and have an ice cream stop. She agreed and sounded excited. I said I would pick her up the next morning. My sleep that night was fitful. By the time the first fingers of light reached out from the eastern horizon, I had had my second cup of coffee. Wondering why I was feeling anxious, I stepped out into the coolness, pulled my collar up and walked to the barn. The skies were without a cloud, a potentially perfect autumn day. I swore that I was going to do my best to keep it that.

Cara was all smiles and giggles when I picked her up. She talked non-stop as we drove back roads, tossing a coin each time we came to a crossroad or a Y. "Heads, to the left, tails, to the right" she would call, then flip that coin. We came across a logging road and Cara suggested we walk it. We hiked upward until the road veered sharply, a point at which a narrow foot trail took off and led to what appeared to be an open ledge. Cara flipped a coin, and we took the narrow foot path and soon reached the ledge. A hewn-timber bench beckoned, and we sat. Balsam fir and hemlock gave way to birch and poplar as the forest floor made a precipitous descent to the ravine below. Below, the ravine gradually broadened into a valley with a meandering stream which stretched eastward to where everything merged into a blue haze.

Cara began to shiver. I pulled an extra flannel shirt from my pack and put it around her shoulders. She laid her head upon my shoulder. When she continued to shiver, we rose and made our way back to the car.

Soon we entered a tiny hamlet consisting of a half-dozen houses and a small store no bigger than a two-car garage.

Tillersville Mega Country Store it said. We laughed, and I pulled up to it. We purchased a few items for lunch, then headed out to find a place that the store clerk had said was a good place to picnic. Cara wasn't saying anything.

"Are you ok?" I asked.

"I'm hungry," she replied.

A few miles out from the village we came across a cleared area with a park bench offering a spot to sit by a stream. "I think this is it," I said. A sign said Conconquin River Picnic Area. We got out and went down to the stream. Cara seemed amused.

"What?" I asked.

"That they call this a river," she said.

I chuckled. "Yeah, I was thinking the same. Like having a country store from which you could load its entire contents into the back of a pickup truck."

She laughed. "Less is more, not?"

I got a blanket from the car, and we sat on the bench and ate. As I ate the last of my sandwich, I noticed that she had taken only two bites from her's.

"You're sure that you're ok?" I asked.

"Yeah."

"Sandwich isn't good?"

"It's ok. I guess I'm not hungry." She laid her head on my shoulder.

I knew she was not ok, and I knew not to push for her to say more.

Later we ran across our ice cream bar. I had a cone. Cara got a banana split, ate half of it and asked if I would eat the rest. As we headed back toward her place she began to talk. For a full hour I listened to accounts of past misfortunes. It seemed to me that an undercurrent of victimization laced every story. By the time we reached her place, I felt exhausted. I declined her invitation to stay. She broke down in tears then. "Please don't be like the rest of them," she said.

I held her until her sobs ceased. "Thank you for spending the day with me. I'm going home and will call you in a day or two. I promise."

five

I wanted to understand. Almost everyone she had mentioned in her accounts of hardships was labeled an asshole. I realized I had not heard her express empathy for anyone since we first met. Nor had I ever heard her say she was sorry. I felt sure that she was thinking that she would not hear from me again. It was all so sad. By the time I arrived at my home, I was exhausted and depressed; all I wanted to do was go to bed.

I called her two days later as promised. She said she did not want to talk, then informed me that I was a narcissistic sociopath.

A few days later she called regarding a medical issue. Her voice was friendly. I recall asking myself, does she even remember telling me that I'm a sociopath?

six

Cara's mother was found to have Placenta Previa in the first week of the third trimester of an unplanned pregnancy. She was put on strict bed rest, however, a week later she began to hemorrhage and was promptly admitted to the hospital. Within an hour of admission, she was wheeled to an operating room.

Baby Cara was extracted via cesarean-section from her mother's womb at 29 weeks gestational age. Upon delivery she was limp, pale, and barely breathing. There was no cry. Her initial apgar (a measure on a scale of 1 - 10 of the physical condition of a newborn at time of delivery) was 2. Apgars of 1 -3 indicate the need for resuscitation. Cara was promptly intubated, hooked up to a ventilator, and whisked to the neonatal intensive care unit.

Being delivered 11 weeks before term produces extreme stress within a very biologically vulnerable and developmentally fragile infant.

During her first hours, after being removed from her mother into a cold and unfamiliar place, with a tube running through her mouth and down her throat into her chest, pushing and extracting air into and from her chest, tiny baby Cara also experienced multiple needle sticks that were necessary to obtain blood and to insert an intravenous line. Following that, placement of a feeding tube through her mouth and into her stomach was done. This was Cara's introduction into the world of humans, and every instance of probing and pain was connected to the touch and handling by human hands; before long a human voice and touch elicited crying.

On her third day Cara was weaned from the ventilator, but within hours she showed signs of deterioration and was promptly hooked back up to the ventilator. An x-ray at that time revealed lung granularity, consistent with respiratory distress syndrome. The following day a cranial ultrasound revealed evidence of bilateral matrix hemorrhages in the brain. On day five Cara was again weaned from the ventilator and held her own with supplemental oxygen under an oxyhood.

Tube feedings were poorly tolerated by her insufficiently developed gastrointestinal tract, resulting in diarrhea and inadequate nutrition. Supplemental intravenous nutrition was added to her regimen, allowing a decrease in the volume given by tube, resulting in less diarrhea.

On day twelve Cara became fussy and began to have episodes of shallow breathing and slowing of her heart rate. Within another hour her abdomen became extended, and shortly thereafter bloody stool was noted. At this point Cara was crying and could not be quieted. Antibiotics were instituted. An abdominal x-ray suggested the possibility of necrotizing enterocolitis (infected bowel resulting in non-viable bowel tissue). Tiny baby Cara was then taken to the Operating Room and abdominal exploratory surgery confirmed necrotizing enterocolitis. Excision of the necrotic tissue resulted in removal of 2/3rds of her small bowel. The post-op course was tenuous. Within a day of discontinuing antibiotic coverage Cara developed sepsis, and broad-spectrum antibiotic coverage was again instituted.

seven

Four weeks after her initial surgery Cara underwent a second surgical operation during which an additional amount of small bowel as well as the proximal portion of the ascending colon were excised. An anastomosis of the remaining small bowel to the remaining colon was successfully accomplished. From that point it was a two-steps-forward, one-step-backward struggle that continued for many months. Long-term intravenous hyperalimentation (artificial supply of nutrients via veins) is always challenging, and at such a level of prematurity will induce additional complications. Repeatedly baby Cara developed sepsis. Each such event was life threatening. The high level of stress due to illness plus that of frequently inflicted pain associated with needle sticks and incisions, threatened to completely overwhelm the child's immunological competence. Odds were against survival – as they had been since her first days.

But Cara gradually grew stronger.

Her story became known throughout the medical center community. A pediatric nurse who was involved with Cara's care since the infant's second week, said "I don't believe there was a single night I did not pray for that precious one. I will never ever forget her."

eight

It was a beautiful early May morning when baby Cara was discharged from the hospital on her 268th day of life. The event was not only beautiful but was noteworthy for the fanfare and flowers. Joyful yet tearful goodbyes were said, as Cara was delivered into in the arms of a woman that she barely recognized but would eventually know to be her mother. As the child and her parents got into their car and drove away, staff members placed a hand over their heart with fingers crossed for tiny Cara.

Cara was re-hospitalized multiple times over the months following her initial discharge. Infections were numerous and minor surgical procedures were necessary for the maintenance of ongoing intravenous nutritional support. Over the course of the next six months Cara was weaned off the intravenous feeding as frequent small feedings via a stomach-tube proved adequate for weight-gain. Daily visits by a nurse assured that the mother/child relationship was holding up adequately and that feedings were done as instructed. Cara was two-and-a-half years old by the time she was able to continue adequate growth without the stomach-tube. Hospitalizations and emergency room visits steadily decreased over the following years. However, the gastrointestinal challenges of a "short gut" with its ongoing symptoms of abdominal cramping, bloating, and diarrhea, continually plagued Cara and would likely be for her the norm for the rest of her life.

Inherited genetic abnormalities resulting in structural defects further challenged her as she grew older. These along with the gastrointestinal problems made it difficult to join other kids in their various activities.

nine

      Cara's most painful memories of her youth are those of her mother's constant ridicule. Cara learned early that she was not pleasing to her parents, that she was not good enough. Endless were her mother's complaints of how much time she was in the bathroom, of how smelly the bathroom always was, and how her constant farting stank up the house. When Cara became of school age, her mother's disapproval was expanded to such things as the clothes Cara chose to wear, and of the way she wore her hair. Cara recalls overhearing her mother complain to relatives that she was embarrassed to be seen with her daughter. When Cara wasn't at school, she would spend most of her time in her bedroom - to avoid hearing her mother's hurtful comments.

School life was no better. Cara had to ask permission to go to the restroom frequently. It was not long until her teacher reported to the school principal that Cara was using her physical condition as an excuse to escape class time, nor did her teacher refrain from making comments regarding the situation in the presence of classmates. Constantly teased, Cara's academic and social difficulties increased. When the school principal spoke to her parents regarding her worsening performance, Cara's parents scolded her for being lazy. Cara was subsequently moved to a special-ed classroom.

ten

When Cara reached puberty, new challenges emerged. Vaginal bleeding occurred without warning and at times was heavy enough to overwhelm a double pad. Her mother denied Cara's medical condition, so Cara turned to her grandmother.

Cara shares a memory of how she and another girl were invited by a guy whom she liked a lot, to join him and his best friend to watch a documentary on the Beatles. He had just obtained a new car and said he would pick them up. During the ride Cara unknowingly bled sufficiently to get through onto the fabric of the front seat. The boy was furious, screaming that she was a freak. The boy's father called Cara's mom and said she would be held liable for the cost of restoration of the seat. The following day at school was horrible. But what hurt

Cara most was that her mom refused to talk to her for a week afterward.

Cara grew to accept there was no way she could ever win her mother's approval. She realized that her mother would never get over having had that unplanned pregnancy that gave her an "impossible daughter" whom she was ashamed of.

eleven

Cara's best friend during her school years was her grandma, whom she visited as often as allowed. Cara's mom increasingly restricted how often Cara was able to go. Thus, Cara's bedroom continued to be the safest place for her to hang out. She went through the Sears & Roebuck catalog cover-to-cover many times.

Cara liked her older sister Janine, but there was a seven-year age difference and Janine didn't have much time for her. Janine did well in sports and was a popular girl. Seeing the attention her sister received, Cara chose to play in school sports as well, but because of impairments, she never succeeded in the ways her sister did. Instead, Cara was accused of not trying hard enough and not caring. Cara gets teary eyed when she talks about it, saying that she tried her hardest. It seemed nothing she did was good enough for the others to want to include her. No one was aware of her first year of life, no one recognized that Cara has poor muscular coordination as well as visual difficulties related to both structural and neurological anomalies.

.

twelve

Cara became more and more a loner. Coming to grips with the fact that her life could never be normal, she wondered if it was worth it - the never-ending struggle, the dismissals without explanation, the glances, the awful feeling each time a person appeared to go out of their way to avoid her. But Cara clung to one hope: that she would one day have a boyfriend.

Then came the day that her doctor told her that she could never have a child, for she would not survive it. He refused to provide birth-control pills and instructed her that she must accept her fate and never have intercourse.

"So much for ever having a boyfriend," Cara said as I topped off our coffee, "It was music, long walks, and Grandma, that account for my being here today."

thirteen

During her senior year in high school, Cara's new English teacher realized Cara was exceptional in literary proficiency. She encouraged Cara to go to college and promised to assist in the application process. Within two months Cara was accepted into a state college. Her college years were lonely years, studies demanding all of her time; easily distracted and challenged in maintaining attention, she had to read a paragraph many times for it to sit in her mind unjumbled. But once that was accomplished, her memory of words, names, and lyrics was astounding.

fourteen

It was a cold day in late November. Already the world was white and ponds iced over. I was sipping coffee when I received a text message from Cara saying she wanted to drop by to return something she had borrowed. I replied that that was fine. Two months had passed since the day we had had lunch by the Conconquin River. I had concluded that I'd probably not see her again. A few hours later, upon hearing the dog bark, I glanced up to see Cara's Chevy tackling the lane. As I rose to put tea on, I received a call from my brother Craig. "Just called to say Mom died early this morning," he said, "I'll get back to you regarding plans."

It wasn't a surprise; Mom had suffered a major stroke two months earlier. Still, it walloped me. I turned the stove off and sat down. Mom had been a best friend.

For fifty years I had called her every Saturday morning.

Cara knocked and entered the cabin with a cheerful "Hi, how are you?" then paused, looked at me, and asked "What's wrong?"

"Mom died."

Cara said nothing, set her bag down and pulled out her cell phone. The thought that Mom would never answer the phone again crashed upon me. I buried my face in my hands and cried. Cara muttered something and walked out the door. I heard the Chevy start up and pull away.

fifteen

A month after mom's passing, I put the farm on the market. It sold instantly. I agreed to move out within two weeks. Cara showed up at my door as I was packing.

"Come on in," I said.

"Where are you going?" she asked.

I told her I sold the farm, and that I would probably reside at my brother Jon's place for a spell.

"I can't believe you did that!" she said in exasperation, "Why? I thought we were going to stay and make it work! You need to not do this! Tell them you changed your mind!"

"Cara, I sold it. It's a done deal. I cannot reverse it."

"Why not? It's your place, just tell them!" She began to unpack a suitcase, then broke into tears.

"Cara, it is not my farm to sell. It now belongs to someone else."

"Ok," she said. "Would you like some coffee?"

"Sure, coffee sounds good."

She smiled and headed for the kitchen. I was envious that she could do that - reverse on the dime. We sat by the east window then, sipping espresso, watching the goats hanging out in the barnyard. Snow-covered pastures stretched to the woodlands. I finished my coffee and rose. Cara sighed, looked up at me and said, "You can stay with me instead of going to Jon's, if you like."

sixteen

I learned that Cara was thirty-one. I remember thinking it was funny that anything between 15 and 50 would have been believable. One minute she would be revealing the wisdom of an elder, and the next minute she would say or do something that I thought normal for a ten-year old.

Cara sees life in extremes. She may see me as a super friend today, and tomorrow I may be trash. A middle ground does not appear on her map. Gradually I realized that she lacked a sense of another's degree of constancy. If someone she knew was seen as a good and considerate person, but today did or said something that she took as being purposely hurtful, he or she was despicable and dangerous.

seventeen

It was a blustery mid-winter night, one of those 'Nor'easter' storms with howling winds that drive snow horizontally. Windows in Cara's little apartment rattled with every gust, cold drafts seemed to come from every direction. Cara was in the lounge chair with a heavy wool blanket pulled snuggly about her. I had put on an extra flannel shirt. But the extra did little to make us feel warmer, for the storm inside the apartment was worse than that out in the darkness. Stinging words rattled our souls. Cara had unleashed an all-too-familiar verbal thrashing, and before long I had yielded to yelling. I caught myself then and went silent. Cara waged on for another half minute then stopped mid-sentence.

"Cara, I am sorry," I said, "I do not want to fight."

"Thank you for your apology," she replied coolly. "I'm going to take a shower now." I watched her disappear into the bathroom. A moment later I grabbed my coat and duffel bag, and left the apartment.

I had no idea where I was going. I was nearing my car a block away when I heard her calling out. I turned to see her running toward me through the driving snow in slippers and gym shorts, clutching an unbuttoned shirt, crying out for me to please come back. Dropping my duffel, I ran to her and carried her back to her apartment. I for a moment struggled with what to do, then grabbed the wool blanket and wrapped it about her and held her to me. She said she wished to lie down. I laid a comforter doubled on the floor. I said that I had to go fetch my duffel bag. She was sobbing, saying over and over that she loved me, that she was sorry. Clinging to my arm, she pleaded with me to promise that I would not sneak off again after she fell asleep. I promised, retrieved my duffel, then lay beside her. We fell asleep on the floor in each other's arms.

It was early dawn when I awoke. She was still clinging onto my arm. The dawn, it seemed, brought light back into our world.

We sat together by the window, sipping coffee. Presently she touched my arm and pointed toward the old pine in the back yard. "Joe and Suze," she said. My mind shot back to the night we had dinner at Anjour's seven months earlier. Those seven months felt like years.

eighteen

.

It was six months after having sold the farm that I found the cabin I would end up buying. I took Cara to see it. She immediately wanted me to buy it, insisted that I call the agent immediately. "I usually go slow on things like the purchase of a property," I said. She got out her phone, saying "I'll call."

"Don't," I said.

"Will you call tomorrow? I want to live with you here," she said.

Two weeks later I signed the papers to make the cabin mine. Cara and I agreed that I would sleep in the cabin loft and she would get the bedroom.

nineteen

When Cara is in conversation with a person she has just met, she is all there - attentive and responsive. The talk is lite and pleasant - and it is where Cara's incredible memory and conversational skill is revealed. She receives compliments such as "well, you certainly are a smart girl! It's been nice chatting with you."

That is the fuel that keeps her going.

Initially coming across as super intelligent can make things volatile when the new acquaintance becomes a co-worker or employer or housemate; they find themselves dealing with a person who is so easily distracted that an agreement - or instruction, is distorted if not simply lost. I have witnessed Cara upon starting a new job, step forth with a positive attitude and a front of confidence, yet within 15 minutes of having received instruction, she appears to have forgotten that instruction; in her brain it has become jumbled. Supervisors who are not aware of her challenges assume she is not sincere. When it is pointed out that she is not doing as instructed, Cara becomes defensive and retorts with the likes of "You didn't make it clear enough" or "you didn't tell me that." It does not take long until her supervisor no longer wants to deal with her, and as often as not she is fired or transferred. Confused and frustrated, she realizes again that she is seen as inadequate to fill the position, even though it may be menial work that she knows she can do.

What I see is that she does not know what to do when her brain is failing her.

For Cara then, every employment becomes extremely stressful, and every employer or supervisor ends up being an "asshole". We have talked about these struggles. Sometimes she just does not want to talk. Sometimes she becomes tearful, and I attempt to reassure her that she is, despite her difficulties, appreciated. I explain that many times the other person does not intend to be mean, that they are simply uncomfortable and do not have the skills to navigate a problem they do not understand. Reminding her of that seems to help, yet Cara tires easily during such conversations and is quick to withdraw, often retreating to her bed and disappearing under the covers.

It does not help that Cara avoids making eye contact, and when she does, it is for a split second. She admits that she does not see faces. She is embarrassed when she fails to recognize a person with whom she had conversed the day prior.

She becomes tearful when we talk about this.

twenty

It was a beautiful autumn morning, skies clear, horizons sharp and seemingly closer than usual. Cara had arrived the day prior, and I was excited to be with her again; it had been six months since I had last seen her. We sipped coffee by the window overlooking the garden. She was unusually quiet. I thought to suggest that we hike the trail leading to the top of Elsey Mountain, it being so beautiful outside, but held back. I watched a raven lite on a high branch of the tall, dead, northern pine between us and the garden, then swoop down to land smoothly on the compose pile beneath. Cara shifted on her stool, then asked in little more than a whisper, "Can we go for a hike this morning?" I replied that it was an excellent idea. "I would like to do the trail on Elsey Mountain," she said. I smiled, always a bit stunned because of how often she appeared to read my mind. Within an hour we were on the road, and fifteen minutes later we pulled into the parking area at the foot of the trail. Cara had remained quiet, and I did not pry.

We were near the summit when she suggested we step off the trail to enjoy the view from her secret ledge, a small open space not more than eight by four feet, well hidden from the trail; she loved to visit it every time we hiked that trail. For long minutes then we gazed in silence upon the picture-postcard scene below, a quilt of fields and woodlots, and here and there buildings of working farms. Cara took my hand then, something I could not recall her having done before.

"Is it possible that your beliefs are your most fierce enemy?" she asked.

I sucked in my breath to slowly let it out as I kicked a pebble and watched it go over the lip of the ledge. Totally off-guard, I shifted from one foot to the other a few times, speechless; it wasn't the question, but rather that I had never heard her utter something as profoundly philosophical and personal. My eyes grew misty as it hit me just how much I had come to love her. I peered across the expanse below to the ridgeline in the distance, and somewhere in

those timeless moments I heard myself
reply, "Yes, Cara, I think that may be true."

twenty-one

I enjoy taking Cara out to dinner, for she is always very up for it, always excited. On the way she will tell me of restaurants that she has tried and really enjoyed…. until the wait-staff would treat her poorly. She does not understand why people become mean to her. I understand why waiters become short with her. Cara has tremendous difficulty choosing when offered choices. Selecting from a restaurant menu is for her a major challenge. I have watched her struggle – it is a back-and-forth, back-and-forth, and it drags on until the waiter becomes visibly irritated. At times I venture the risk of stepping in and help her decide. She has become used to hearing a casual comment from me a bit later saying I think her decision was a good one. It seems to work; she smiles and says "Yay!"

twenty-two

It was a mid-October afternoon a year later when I glanced out the window and saw Cara pulling into my drive. I had not heard from her in many months. I watched as she gathered her bags. I stepped outside, welcomed her, and took her bags.

"Coffee?" I asked.

"Of course!" she replied.

As we sat, I said, "Skye and I missed you." She looked at me.... and held her gaze, and I thought Wow! a first! a change! As if she read my mind, she laughed, and so did I. She handed me a card. It said Happy Anniversary! I looked at her, perplexed.

"It was four years ago today I showed up to buy a banjo," she said, "and you slayed me."

"I what??"

"You slayed me.... you captured me."

We sat in silence then, sipping coffee, staring out over the garden and woodlands. I wondered if I would ever know if I was a positive influence in her life. As if she read my thoughts, she set down her cup and turned to me and said, "I want to tell you that I think you understand me better than any other person in my life." She returned her gaze toward the gardens. "The coffee is good," she said.

"Thank you, Cara."

Cara suggested we go for a walk. "The sunset will be beautiful!"

"Sounds good," I said, "let's walk down the road past Sara's."

"Yay!" she replied as she grabbed another cookie.

Down the road apiece, as I pointed to a patch of wild lupine, we stopped abruptly. A cow moose was headed our way, coming across the field at an easy lope. It appeared she had not seen us yet. Cara slipped up against me as the moose reached the road about thirty yards ahead, stopped halfway across the road and swung her head to stare at us. After a moment the moose resumed an easy lope on into the next field and a minute later entered the woods beyond. The setting sun had slipped down behind distant mountains. Cara laid her head on my shoulder. Neither of us uttered a word - perhaps because no words were adequate.

As we walked back toward home, Cara stopped and pointed to one of a few small billowy clouds still visible in the fading western sky. "Look! That cloud looks like a fish!" she exclaimed.

I laughed. "Yes, it does!"

We watched as it slowly faded into the deepening dusk. I noticed Cara shivering. I draped my extra flannel shirt around her shoulders. "Let's go home," I said. "I'll make tea."

twenty-three

Where Cara was raised, if it snowed, it was a few inches and would be gone within a day. Nonetheless their schools would close for the day. Here in the north country the world is white five months of the year, and schools *may* close if a blizzard is wreaking havoc. I shared with Cara tips on driving in snow, what not to do and what to try for, assuring her that with practice she would become comfortable driving during winter. Her car was an old VW wagon, and it wasn't an all-wheel-drive vehicle. I advised she buy snow treads, but she procrastinated on that. Shortly after that we had an early November snow, and it was dumping more than had been expected. Cara called as dusk was settling in, saying she was in Clarkston and wondered if she could stay the night at my place. I replied that she was welcome and said that I'd meet her at the bottom of the hill, because unless the plow had just gone through, it was unlikely she would make it up. Fifteen minutes later as I was slowly making my way down the mile-long hill, she appeared coming around a bend, already a third of the way up. The ole VW was barely crawling, slipping to the side a little here-and-there, but still climbing. I was awed that she had made that far. At the bottom of the hill, I turned around and headed back up, figuring she was likely to be hung up by the time I reached her. The challenge would be to get her car turned around without getting hit by a vehicle coming downhill. I was astonished to find that she was three-quarters of the way up and still moving. The front end of the VW slipped toward the ditch every time she broke traction, but each time she expertly pulled out of that and kept inching her way to the top. I was stunned, and incredibly proud of her. When we arrived at my place, I hugged her. She was trembling, but she had a big smile on that beautiful face. "I am totally impressed," I said, "and very proud of you!" I could see in her eyes that she needed that - so very much.

twenty-four

Cara's next visit came some months later. I sensed a change right off. It wasn't long until our exchange took a sudden nosedive. After delivering a brutal verbal attack, she grabbed her bags and drove off. I was wordless; none of it made any sense to me. Her words were daggers, and I was bleeding.

Over the following years most visits were short. Sudden, unannounced departures became the norm. I would wake in the morning to hear her car start, rise to see her throwing her belongings into her car and drive off. There was never a note explaining her departure. I was unable to connect it with something said. Often months would pass without correspondence. I never knew if I would ever see her again.

It has been said that if one is totally receptive, they will see that for everything that is given, something is likewise taken away or is dropped.

Perhaps there is a limit to what can be carried.

Unlike those of us who at times simply refuse to consider a middle ground, Cara appears unable to see that a middle ground exists. I am not sure why it took me so long to understand that Cara cannot see me as I am. It is vital that I see and understand this, for what, when suddenly I am in her eyes all bad, is there for her to hang onto?

twenty-five

It was a late-summer day, and I was making applesauce. The kitchen was like a sauna. On top of that everything seemed to be going wrong. So when I saw Cara's car pulling up to the cabin, I realized that I had mixed feelings about her unannounced visit. But soon she was helping me make applesauce. It wasn't long until I corrected her when she failed to follow directions. A tirade of degrading accusations followed until I lost it and was yelling. I angrily kicked an open cupboard door by which she was squatting, and it nipped her knee as it slammed shut. She cried out, saying I hurt her. Stunned by what I had just done, I examined her knee, saw no mark, and knew that it was her heart that I had injured. I apologized, telling her that hurting her was not something I wanted to do, and that I would go, for I had violated us. I rose then, got my jacket, and left the cabin.

I drove then for hours through blinding tears, not knowing where to go, what to do, and unable to forgive myself. It began to rain heavily and before long I found myself barely able to see as blackness fell. I stopped at the first motel, exhausted and half wishing I had the guts to take my life.

twenty-six

The following day I crossed the state line, heading westward with no idea where I was going. Around noon Cara called, her voice weak, "Please come back," she pleaded. I said I could not. I kept driving.

It was dusk when I ran upon a state park and without thought turned in, glad for the camping gear I keep in the car. For the next three days I did nothing but sit at my campsite. I told myself that I was a sad and colossal failure. I told myself that I had to remove myself from her life, perhaps from everyone's life. I was scared. How did I get to this? As I turned in that night, I asked myself, what would I suggest to a self-destructive other. I would tell them to get their body moving and keep it moving, that that would help them rise above the quagmire. It would free them of the undertow that could steal them from people who did not want to lose them, from people who needed them even.

I set out the next morning at the break of dawn, determined to hike all day. I pushed hard, as if I had to reach some point by day's end to save my life. The sun was setting in the west when I collapsed onto a bed of pine needles at the base of a huge Northern pine.

I woke as a new dawn ushered in a new day. It was a beautiful morning, and I lay there taking in birdsong, the smell of pine, and a promising sky. The heaviness I had carried the prior day seemed to have dissipated. Upon rising I was shocked at how stiff and sore I was. I began walking and eventually came upon a pond. The sun appeared to be midway to noon though the air still held a chill. I sat at the water's edge, dipped my blistered feet into its cool welcome. I watched mayflies scoot about on smooth water. The sun was warm upon my face. I laid back on the grass and closed my eyes. I asked the gods and goddesses to have the sun shine its warmth on Cara as well. It was then that I sensed a darkening and felt the sun's warmth slip away. I opened my eyes to see that a singular cloud had formed overhead. Within moments that cloud opened its belly and drenched me, then stopped as abruptly as it had started. The cloud soon vaporized into nothingness. A pair of yellow finches fed but a few feet away. I spoke to them. I sat up, totally soaked, and started laughing. I turned to the finches and whispered, "Thank you." They cocked their little heads then, and in absolute synchronicity flitted up and away. The sky was as clear as it had been earlier. I rose and headed toward camp, realizing how hungry I was, yet upon reaching my campsite, I promptly broke camp, threw my gear in the back of the car, and headed back the way I had come. I knew that she would be gone when I got back, yet I drove into and through the night. As the miles slipped by, questions flooded me: Am I delusional to believe I know myself better than others know me? Am I able to see the lie and the arrogance in thinking that the way I see the world, or my relationship with Cara, is the way it is?

twenty-seven

I woke to the howl of a wolf. The clock said 1:30 a.m. I thought of Cara and her stories about her encounters with wolves during her work at the Wrengell-St. Elias National Park. I thought of Deena, the Navajo RN who was my assistant at the Fort Defiance Hospital serving the Navajo. Deena spoke of those who can in the night take on the form of wild animals such as a wolf, sometimes with nefarious intent. That howl, so close...... Cara? I chuckled at myself, then sat up on the side of the bed. It had been four months since I last heard from her. That last day I had been with her, the day I kicked the cupboard door, the day I ran away..... what did that do to her? I crawled back under the covers, wondering if I could ever forgive myself.

I rose at six, got a fire going in the wood stove, made coffee, and remembered that it was my birthday. Cara had never missed my birthday, always made it a wonderful day. I knew that I would probably never hear from her again. From my window I watched a gust kick up a whirl of snow and funnel it halfway across the field. I poured a second cup of coffee. I hoped she was ok. The lonely cry of a wolf came again. She's back again, I said to myself. I grabbed my coat and stepped outside. The thermometer read -2 F. I peered around the corner, squinting to see the woods to the north, but the wind had snow swirling to the point of a near whiteout, making the distant tree line nearly invisible. I stepped back inside and went to the kitchen window, scanning the edge of the woods as the wind ebbed.

I can't say how long I stood there, but a knock on the door jerked me around. I grabbed my snub-nose Colt 32 just in case as I went to the door, wondering who the hell would be here in this weather; the closest neighbor was nearly a mile away. I swung the door open. "Happy Birthday!" Cara exclaimed, dropping her bag and throwing her arms around me. I pulled her inside, grabbing her bag.

"Thanks so much, Cara," I whispered coarsely, fighting back tears. I could see that she was shivering uncontrollably. I pulled her to me and grabbed a blanket.

"Toast and coffee?" I asked.

"Of course!"

Cara asked if it was ok if she stayed for a few days. I replied that I wished it could be more, and she giggled like the little girl she could so easily be at times. If I ever had a better birthday, I couldn't remember it.

twenty-eight

The few days turned into weeks. I was happy and she appeared to be likewise. The time together reassured us that we were ok, and that we would continue to care about the other. We had accomplished changes.... remarkable, I thought, for an old man and a deeply scarred survivor bearing a load of "disorders".

It was during the 6th week of her stay that Cara received a message informing her that she had been awarded a position at a National Park in New Mexico. She was to start work in three weeks. She said she would drive out rather than fly. I suggested she allow several days extra for the trip.

On the last day of that visit, as she was packing, Cara paused, came over and sat on my knee, and laid her head on my shoulder. "I love you," she whispered. Then she cried. With tears streaming down my cheeks, I held her tight. Had a bomb struck outside, I may not have noticed.

"You have Kleenex?" she asked, smiling through beautiful tears.

"No Kleenex. But there's toilet paper," I replied.

We laughed.

twenty-nine

A year passed. I received from Cara
two or three emails during the first month,
then it dropped off to but the briefest reply
to the occasional note that I would send. I
was hurt a bit, though not surprised, and so
gradually I quit sending 'Are you ok?'.

Another year passed. I received a
Christmas card and a Birthday card. I
wondered if she remembered me other than
when reminded by a calendar. I feared that I
would never see her again. I think that was
the loneliest and most grey year of my seven
decades. That winter the flu nearly took me
out.

thirty

Skye pulled hard on her leash, the wind furiously whipping funnels of snow across open fields. "Let's go home," I said, patting her head. My cell phone went off then, and though I thought to not answer, I did.

"Hi, how are you?" It was Cara, her voice weak and trembling.

"Cara! What's up? Are you ok?"

"I'm ok…. I guess."

"Where are you?"

"I'm in Tillersville."

"Tillersville!"

"Remember the bench by the river where we had lunch?"

"Of course, I remember! Are you in trouble?"

"No, I'm ok, just upset and don't know what I ….."

Silence. I saw we were disconnected. Poor signal was the norm for where I was. I sent a text saying that I would call when I reached the cabin.

It was an hour later I called her. She sounded terrible but refused to give a direct answer when I asked what was wrong. Instead, she informed me that she wished to buy or rent the neighboring cabin adjacent to my property and wondered if I would contact the owner and inquire if that was something he would consider. "Afterall, nobody has been living there, right?"

I was stunned. "Yes, Cara, most of the time there's nobody there, but he does rent it out on occasion during summer. And he stays there during deer season."

"So will you contact him?"

"Cara, this makes no sense to me. You hate the long cold winters up here, and you don't like living where it's this rural because of all the driving you do to maintain a social life. So what's the deal?"

She was silent for a few moments, then blurted "Why are you like this? You know I can't afford the rent that most apartments are going for. You know the problems I deal with when living in shared quarters, because of my health problems, and how important good sleep is for me. I have managed to save some money. I wish to live close to you, to learn more of your homesteading skills, and more about gardening. It's probably the only way I can afford to live alone and take care of myself with these health problems."

Knowing her proclivity to act on impulse and then lose interest after action has been taken, I informed her that I wanted to give this a bit of thought.

On the following morning I told her that I would contact Mr. McMann and tell him of her interest in buying or renting the cabin.

"Yay!" was all she said.

thirty-one

McMann said he would sell. There was a lot of repair work to be done. I assumed that Cara's parents had agreed to help her purchase it. I messaged Cara, asking her to drive up so that we could discuss this in person. She replied that she would within the week.

thirty-two

.

I turned and saw Cara's VW pulling into my drive. I dropped my tools and walked over to greet her. I stopped when I saw that she sat in her car with her head resting on the steering wheel. After a few moments she raised her head, opened the door and got out, hanging onto the door and looking wobbly on her feet. Her face was gaunt, had dark circles around her eyes, and though she had always been skinny, she now looked like a skeleton. I gasped, ran over to her and took her into my arms. She was trembling like a tiny, captured bird. With her face buried against my neck, she whispered "Hi." Knowing that the last thing she wanted in that moment was questions, I said "Let's have tea." She weakly smiled, nodding, and we stepped inside. I draped a throw around her shoulders and moved a small heater close by. We sipped tea in silence. I asked her if she wished to take a nap.

"Yes, I would like that," she said.

Cara informed me she would pay McMann's price, yet soon I learned that she possessed only half the asking price. She said she would get the remainder, that she had two friends who said they would loan her money. I asked how well she knew them, and she did not answer. I soon realized there was no way she was able to buy the cabin and not lose it along the way. I suggested we take Skye for a walk, to which she agreed. Putting a hand to her shoulder, I said "And perhaps while we walk, you can tell me about the last two years."

Cara said that she had been doing fine during the first months on the job in New Mexico, but when she complained about the park's housing being untenable for one with her health problems, the Park Manager seemed uninterested and simply informed her that no other living space could be provided. A day later the Park Manager called her into his office and informed Cara that her supervisor complained that her bathroom breaks were increasingly frequent, and that sometimes she was in that bathroom for fifteen minutes. The supervisor had also stated that he was often re-doing things where Cara had failed to follow instructions. Cara informed the manager that the supervisor failed to give adequate instructions, and that her co-workers weren't doing their jobs and were putting the blame on her. When the Park Manager accused Cara of exaggerating and passing the blame, Cara 'let him have it', and was fired.

The day after, Cara met Ben, who, upon hearing her story, invited her to move in with him, offering room and board in exchange for helping around the house. Ben reminded Cara of her dad, and she liked him…. and trusted him. Cara moved in with Ben the next day. For the first few months she was happy being with Ben. Ben was the boyfriend she had been waiting for. Ben willingly accompanied her on a trip to see her parents. Her parents approved of Ben. They had always disapproved of her male friends, so the fact that they liked Ben was incredibly reassuring to her, and she thought that she had finally achieved the life that she had feared she could never know. As months passed however, Ben increasingly declined Cara's invitations to join her in some of their favorite activities. Before long they did very little together. Unable to admit that she was losing him, she rationalized his behaviors as revelations of his own problems. She would, she decided, love him just the same and it would all work out. But Ben's distance only increased. She said she tried to be strong yet found herself crying. She began seeing a therapist. After several months the therapist informed her that she could not help her unless she was willing to accept some responsibility for the way things were falling apart. She said that Cara kept potential love at a distance by unconsciously projecting her own unacceptable traits and behaviors onto the other, and that unless she was willing to consider this insight, little progress would be seen. Cara angrily responded that it was she who knew nothing about love, that she was a terrible therapist.

That was the end of therapy.

Cara felt deserted and alone. She decided that Ben had become a sick man, mired in his own cauldron of anger and insecurities, and that she had to leave him. When she told him she was leaving, he without looking up mumbled "That's fine." Cara ran to her room and cried. She woke at four in the morning and began packing. "I didn't know what to do but go back to live with mom and dad, but then I remembered that you had always said that your door remains open."

thirty-three

As Cara and I left the lawyer's office, she turned to me and said, "Thank you." I smiled, nodding, then peered down at the iced-over stream as we crossed over the bridge, wondering if I had just done the stupidest thing ever.

thirty-four

I promptly began the repairs
necessary for her to start moving in, waiting
for her to call or show up, for we had agreed
to do the work together. It would be a great
learning opportunity for her as a property
owner. When I did not hear from her over
the next three weeks, I found myself
increasingly annoyed. Still another week
passed without a word from her, and I
became depressed. Yet another week and I
threw down my tools and vowed to do no
further work on her cabin.

I sat my coffee down and leaned
back in the rocker, watching Skye eye the
squirrel that she had chased up a tree so
many times. I was doing my best to not to
worry about how this cabin venture was

going to pan out. Regretting that I had spent nearly half of my life savings to help her buy property was now slowly undoing me. As I sat wallowing in an amalgam of resentment, Cara called.

"I thought it's likely that you'd have an update on how things are going at the cabin," she said, "but it seems you're in line with the phrase 'no news is good news', so if that is how you prefer, I will go about my day and let you continue whatever it is you're working on. It seems you aren't too eager to communicate, but I guess you're busy. I must pick up an item in Waterbury and thought I could then head on up to your place, but if you want to be alone…."

After long moment of silence, I replied "I do not wish to see you."

"Are you mad at me?"

"You are not a true friend."

"Why do you think this? I thought you would be happy to see me. Why are you being so degrading and mean?"

"Cara, I suggest you take time to reflect on this long enough to have some idea why I said what I did. I am going to hang up now. Goodbye."

thirty-five

She would come back at me, I knew, slinging accusations and anything else she could come up with to destroy any sense of self-worth I may have; it's just what she always did went she felt that she was being blamed or in some way diminished.

Her response came via email.
'You are taking advantage of me. You see my medical conditions and say you want to help me, but your manipulative behavior shows that you really do not care for me. You continue to try to disenfranchise me, despite my conditions. You need to stop trying to manipulate me. You are going back on your word of being a friend. You are trying to make me work for you for free so that you can then verbally and emotionally manipulate and abuse me. You want to have access to me. You are toxic and undependable. My family knows you

physically abused me and are taking advantage of me financially while I have medical problems and am unemployed. Now you are trying again your push-and-pull game so that you can continue to abuse me verbally and emotionally. It is very clear some part of you is very, very sick. I continue to forgive you and try to see the good inside of you. I try to think your anger will dissipate. You've chosen not to include me about my new home. If you don't wish to help me do what needs to be done on my home, I know that Nancy will gladly list it on the MLS. Now is the time to begin advertising this. It is appalling that I have not even gotten to see it yet, but then, in your misogynistic fashion you say you don't wish to see me... well, I must move on. Stop with the BS. Let's list this for more than we paid for it, I know the market will bear it. Or you can just hand the property over to me since you've sought to disenfranchise me and abuse me for 5 years, including getting my family involved and you threatening my property and personal safety multiple times. If you don't recall these events because of your cognitive dissonance, bipolarism, borderline personality disorder, your PTSD from your youth and the trauma of your ex-wife's accident, or any other situation that is affecting your mental health, then that is not my problem. I will be gone, I will not be updating you on how I'm doing, because you will take advantage of me, including verbal and emotional abuse. I want peace of mind. Let me know if you will hand this property over to me, and I can get it on the market.'

It was pretty much the same that I'd received in times past. That it is a childhood strategy that remains the default doesn't seem to help. On one occasion, several hours after such a fusillade some years earlier, I asked her if she remembered saying such-and-such. She said she did not. I believed her - that she did not recall any of it.

thirty-six

    I was not surprised when two days later I received a flurry of messages saying she was sorry, and that she needs to know what to do. It was what followed every time she had taken her sword and gone after my jugular. I sent the following response:

    Cara, we as individuals do well to remember that where we are today is, at least in part, the result of choices we have made along the way. You, I, and everyone, needs to own that. I do not think I am better than you. I do not need anything you have. I am not responsible for you. I DO, however, care about you. I do worry about your well-being, and I do miss you when you're gone. However, what you again accused me of via emails two days ago is flat-out inexcusable. Own that. Don't even try to defend it. I hope that boundary is now clear. Assassinating

another's character in defensiveness and
anger is an absolute no-no for both of us.

Cara responded with something different than anything I had ever heard from her.

Thank you for your email response. I appreciate it and I think you made good points. When I am stressed, I withdraw, and if I feel threatened, my reflex is to draw my sword and swing with all I've got. I am delicate, I don't stand a chance if I don't fight to annihilate. If I say the things you say I do, I am sorry, I really am. If you wish to know how you stress me, it boils down to this: when I depend on you, I get hurt. I should not have to explain myself or feel shut down, especially when I feel you don't truly know where I'm coming from and are basing your judgment and criticism upon your experiences, which are often vastly different than mine. I don't want to feel like my opinion, feelings, emotions, needs, choices, and experiences are invalid. I need

to communicate with you and to feel
understood and respected.

I was stunned. I re-read it again and again. It hit me that the first response was her default, yet this time she then offered something new, something that had to be germinating for some time... months, years even. I was suddenly exuberant. After decades of being avoided, dismissed, and denigrated, Cara, carrying multiple disabilities, was accomplishing changes that many normal folks fail to pull off. It dawned upon me then that she was also revealing her faith in me.

thirty-seven

Cara left yesterday to visit her parents. In the preceding days she was tense and moody, and I surmised that she was likely going over and over just what she could get in her allotted three carry-ons and how to get her car to a storage shed. Her flight was to be on Thursday, so I suggested that she pack luggage on Tuesday and commit to the first or second attempt as final. On Wednesday I would follow her to the car storage unit and bring her back. We would have a meal together that evening, and the next morning we would get up early and I would get her to the airport by 10:30 for her 12:30 departure. She agreed that that was a good plan.

I was not surprised when during the hour drive to the airport she was attempting to re-do her baggage yet again the entire time. I said nothing, knowing that that would only increase her anxiety. Upon arrival at the terminal, I got out of the car, opened her door for her, and then for the next twenty minutes held this-then-that as she worked frantically to get everything in those three travel bags, all the while checking and rechecking for this, then that. At a point when only a dozen items remained on the car seat, I put a hand to her shoulder and suggested that she let them be, and that I would take them back to her cabin. "You're going to be ok, Cara."

She replied "Ok, I'm ready, I'm going to be ok."

"Is it usually like this, Cara?"

"More-or-less." she replied with a wince.

"Would you like for me to help in getting to baggage check-in?"

"No, I'll do ok."

She then threw her arms around me, trembling, and whispered "Thank you for being my friend." She grabbed her luggage and headed toward the terminal door, struggling to keep her bags from falling off the tote, and disappeared into the terminal.

I drove away from that airport terminal with tears blurring my vision.

thirty-eight

I am now seventy-seven. Cara
continues to use the cabin next door as her
'base camp' while doing seasonal stints for
the National Parks Service.

Our exchanges are messages of
warmth and appreciation. When she is here,
I think there are more sunny days than usual.
At times she becomes confused and feels
lost, and then we have a daily exchange for
several days until things are better.
Sometimes I notice that she has not gone
anywhere for several days, and she starts
showing up at my door bringing the simplest
gifts. and then I'll find an excuse to check
her refrigerator, find it completely empty,
and inform her that I must make a trip into
town for groceries, and would she care to
accompany me?

In the process we made sure we
refurnished her refrigerator. It has been
those days that nourish my soul. Those are
the days in which I turn in at the day's end

feeling genuinely good. They confirm to me that my life continues to have purpose; they propel me to take care of myself so that I can continue providing support and reassurance.

In my mind Cara is the true hero, an angel sent, and I am a lucky man to have had her walk into my life; she in innocence brought sunshine to my days, and I am finally at peace with my life.

Angels do not know
that they are an angel,
they do not know it is for them
to bring down a facade
and reveal a fortress of lies.
She may be the challenged one,
a channel opened through affliction,
capable of understanding things
that normal people do not.
Her work is over before she knows it,
and she is unsure what just happened.
She glances nervously about,
suspecting that she should go,
for she had not meant to invade.
The man, he rises to stand
finally upon solid ground,
and is astonished to see
her beautiful wings,
and he weeps.
It is through their struggle
that we are presented
yet another chance.

.

CARA

Let me acknowledge that I never see the whole, not even of what I hold in hand, let me never forget what I learned in my days with you.

Let me hold thoughtfully, let me be tentative, let me be of an open heart, and let me forgive as humbly as you do.

Let me be the autumn leaf hanging on for one more day in blazing color for those whom I love, and then may I fall gently close to you, my beautiful Cara.

According to the World Health Organization, every year approximately 15 million babies are born preterm (before 37 completed weeks gestation), the rates ranging from 5% to 18% over 184 countries. Currently the rate in the U.S. is approximately10%. Very preterm babies (28 - 32 weeks gestation) comprise only 2 -3 % of all preemies. The significance of preterm birth lies in the complications of prematurity. Infants born in the lower range of viable gestational age brackets (Very Preterm and Extremely Preterm) have the highest rate of all complications and the greatest biological vulnerability and neuro-developmental fragility. The highest rate of neurological development normally occurs during the third trimester of pregnancy. Very Preterm infants are born in the early part of the third trimester, thus Very Preterm birth survivors suffer impairments across multiple neurological domains. These survivors are more likely to experience academic difficulties and manifest behavior problems throughout their life. They are many times more likely to develop psychiatric disorders including attention deficit disorder (ADD/ADHD), autism spectrum disorder (ASD), generalized anxiety, depression, and deficits in socio-emotional processing, than full term birth individuals. In general, Very Preterm survivors have a poorer social life, have fewer friends, have less confidence in romantic situations, and tend to see themselves as less attractive. Personal intimate relationships are exceptionally difficult. They are less likely to marry and to have children. Additionally, VPT survivors have a greater incidence of medical problems as adults and have a shorter life expectancy than that of the general population.

Less-than-optimal parenting is one of the triad of chief contributions to the amalgam of deficiencies that VPT survivors suffer. To be fair, one should point out that preterm birth and prolonged hospitalization of the child are highly stressful experiences for parents. It is the monkey wrench thrown into the parenting preparation process. The distress that parents experience tends to stretch from infancy into childhood. It is often accompanied by clinical depression, which affects a mother's adjustment to her child.

Interestingly, many VPT children develop a near genius ability which is usually limited to one area of cognitive function. In Cara's case, it was in literary and language skills.

At the deepest level Cara struggles to be good enough, to be seen as being of value. Unfortunately, many if not most see her as a spoiled brat with a bad attitude, making it almost impossible for her to gain and sustain a healthy self-esteem. It takes a lot of love, re-assurance, and assistance to counter the demeaning behaviors of the bulk of people in our world.

There are thousands of Cara's, and many fall through the cracks and do not receive the support and assistance they deserve. It is up to you and me to change that.